E-Careers

D1544110

Careers in
Online Gaming

Leanne Currie-McGhee

ReferencePoint
Press®

San Diego, CA

© 2020 ReferencePoint Press, Inc.
Printed in the United States

For more information, contact:
ReferencePoint Press, Inc.
PO Box 27779
San Diego, CA 92198
www.ReferencePointPress.com

LIBRARY OF CONGRESS CATALOGING-IN-PUBLICATION DATA

Name: Currie-McGhee, L.K. (Leanne K.), author.
Title: Careers in Online Gaming/by Leanne Currie-McGhee.
Description: San Diego, CA: ReferencePoint Press, Inc., 2020. | Series:
  E-Careers | Audience: Grade 9 to 12. | Includes bibliographical references
  and index. |
Identifiers: LCCN 2018048175 (print) | LCCN 2018049958 (ebook) | ISBN
  9781682826164 (eBook) | ISBN 9781682826157 (hardback)
Subjects: LCSH: Computer games—Design—Vocational guidance. | Computer
  games—Programming—Vocational guidance.
Classification: LCC GV1469.15 (ebook) | LCC GV1469.15 .C87 2020 (print) | DDC
  794.8023--dc23
LC record available at https://lccn.loc.gov/2018048175

Contents

Fun and Games

Online gaming is one of the most popular forms of modern entertainment. Around the world, people turn to their phones, laptops, computers, tablets, or Xboxes to play classic games or to try new ones. As long as people can access the Internet or a computer network, they can play video games at any time and from any place. Those who love puzzles may play *Words with Friends*, challenging other players to back-and-forth word building. Others enjoy *Minecraft*, in which they can build their own worlds and visit the ones that other players create. Still others choose a multiplayer shooter game like *Fortnite*, in which they can compete against others in simulated worlds. With over 125 million online players, *Fortnite* has attracted players, many of whom are teens, who love the concept of fighting for survival on an island.

Online gaming offers something for everyone. There are sports games, adventure games, shooter games, strategy games, games that can be played alone, massively multiplayer online games (MMOGs)—in which people interact with others in a virtual gaming room—games that are played in real time, and games that can be played by taking turns. These games can be accessed using any Internet-enabled electronic device, which has contributed to the sharp growth of the online gaming industry.

A Growing Industry

Online gaming is a branch of the gaming industry that has significantly evolved since 2000, and especially since around 2015. In 2016 alone MMOGs generated an estimated $1.9 billion in North America. Even though these MMOGs are free to play, their parent companies make money by selling players additional items (such as clothes or tools) that enhance their play experience. This, combined with sales from advertisement revenue, made experts predict that global online gaming revenue would grow by $16 billion from 2011 to 2017. Such huge sums reflect the fact that, according to a 2018 report by the Entertainment Software Association, 60 percent of Americans play video games daily, and in 2016 Americans spent roughly $36 billion on video game content, hardware, and accessories.

This growing industry needs more people to work in it, which is an exciting prospect for video game lovers. The wide variety of careers to be had in the online gaming industry range from creative jobs to technical positions to those that are more business focused. On the technical side, programmers and developers are needed to plan and code the games. In the business space, marketing and sales professionals are needed to advertise and grow the companies that produce the games. For the artistic and creatively inclined, gaming companies need graphic artists, writers, and animators to bring to life a game's stories and visuals. Darby McDevitt, a writer for the video game *Assassin's Creed*, loves many aspects of his job. "I love the extensive research we do before we make any new game," he says in an interview with reporter Jason Bay published on the Game Industry Career Guide website. "When we finally dive into production, I am passionate about writing dialog. I love the sound, and feel, and scent of good writing, so I take great care to make every sentence a masterpiece."

A Competitive Field

This industry provides career options for people of all different interests, and it promises to continually grow and develop. However, while the field has expanded, there is significant competition for available jobs, in part because they pay well and so many people are interested in doing the work. Those in the field describe their work as challenging but exciting. Online gaming industry employees must be willing to handle stress, meet tight deadlines, and continuously problem solve. Steve Bowler is a video game designer with Phosphor Games and has more than twenty years'

Careers in Online Gaming

Occupation	Minimum Educational Requirement	2017 Median Pay
Advertising, promotions, and marketing manager	Bachelor's degree	$129,380
Broadcast and sound engineering technician	Postsecondary education	$42,650
Editor	Bachelor's degree	$58,770
Film and video editor, and camera operator	Bachelor's degree	$58,210
Multimedia artist and animator	Bachelor's degree	$70,530
Musician and singer	No formal educational credential	$26.95 per hour
Producer and director	Bachelor's degree	$71,620
Software developer	Bachelor's degree	$103,560
Writer and author	Bachelor's degree	$61,820

Source: Bureau of Labor Statistics, *Occupational Outlook Handbook*, 2019. www.bls.gov.

experience doing different types of animation and design work. In an interview with Lifehacker, Bowler confirms the attractive but difficult nature of the field. "It's one of the most mentally stimulating and rewarding fields I've ever worked in," he says. "It's also caused me the most anxiety and stress. We work very, very hard making the stuff you love."

Although the industry is very competitive, there are ways to stand out among those vying for jobs. For example, when he was young, Dan Posluns programmed his own games on his TI-85 calculator and Apple IIc and went on to develop independent games and post them online. An established game studio noticed the games he posted and offered him a chance to interview for a position. Posluns is a now a video game designer who has worked on top franchises such as *Spore*, *The Simpsons*, *The Sims*, and *LEGO Star Wars*. He has also written code on multiple platforms, including handheld and mobile devices.

The Future of Gaming

People love to play online video games, and those in the industry believe the trend will continue. According to Ukie (UK Interactive Entertainment), a not-for-profit industry organization that represents gaming start-ups and large multinational developers, the global gaming industry provides services to an estimated 2.2 billion to 2.6 billion people. Experts and analysts believe this will only increase, and Newzoo, a company that analyzes trends in digital media and technology, projects that worldwide revenue for the industry will hit $143.5 billion by the end of 2020.

Further advances in technology are also expected to grow the online gaming industry. One such advance is augmented reality, in which a computer-generated image is superimposed on a user's view of the real world (such as in *Pokémon Go*). Another is virtual reality, a computer-generated simulation of a three-dimensional image or environment. These technologies are continuing to develop and will likely become increasingly featured in games, enhancing consumers' gaming experiences. Faster networks and increased availability of the Internet are among other technological advances that will help grow the gaming industry. These and other developments mean that those who love video games and dream of working in this field will surely find many opportunities to do so.

Animator

What Does an Animator Do?

"Being an animator is a cross between Dr. Frankenstein and an actor," explains Tony Ravo, a video game character animator. In an interview with Jason Bay of the Game Industry Career Guide website, he says, "We basically have to animate—which literally means 'give life' to—static drawings or 3D character models. That's the Dr. Frankenstein part. The actor part [involves] giving them personality and purpose so the player cares about the character." Ravo has been animating video game characters for more than two decades. From children's games like *Finding Nemo* to worldwide hits like *Harry Potter and the Chamber of Secrets*, he has animated dozens of characters.

Animators like Ravo create interactive 2-D and 3-D images that move, talk, and react within a game. This begins with drawing the characters or objects on a storyboard. From there animators create 3-D models, using animation software like Autodesk Maya and ZBrush that allow animators to develop a character's look, movement, and behavior. With this

At a Glance

Animator

Minimum Educational Requirements
Associate's degree or relevant experience

Personal Qualities
Creative, collaborative, observant

Working Conditions
Indoors, in an office

Pay
Median salary of $72,820 as of 2017

Number of Jobs
About 73,700 for all types of animators, including video game, as of 2017

Future Job Outlook
Projected 8 percent increase through 2026

kind of software, the characters or objects must be rigged, which means giving them a programmed "skeleton" and ways to control it. This allows animators to develop a character's movements in the software. Then animators create sequences for the character's motions within the game. After building the animation sequences, the animation is exported to a game engine such as Unity, where all components of the game are linked together. At this point, feedback from the designers and quality-assurance team is given to the animators, who will adjust their animation if needed.

Simon Boxer worked on *Armello*, a game developed by the Australian game studio League of Geeks. Boxer initially sketches his ideas on paper before turning them into moving art. Once he is satisfied with his drawing, Boxer uses Photoshop and an interactive pen and pad known as a Wacom tablet to create a digital file of the character. Then he rigs and animates the object in the animation software. He works collaboratively with designers, other animators, and an art director to complete the process and ensure that specs are being met and that his animation will work well with others' animation. Boxer's days vary depending on what he is working on. "Not all of the tasks are glamorous," he says in an interview with This.com, a website focused on life, learning, and careers. "Sometimes you need to be motivated to get everything done in a timely fashion. Other times it's easy to get into the workflow and the day will flash by."

Animators find job satisfaction in the fact that their work is essential to developing a captivating video game. Richard Lico, an animation director with Polyarc, an independent game studio, believes that animation is crucial to a player's involvement in and satisfaction with a game. "Think about something simple like a punch in a fighting game," explains Lico in an interview on 80 Level, a website about the gaming industry. "How satisfying that punch feels as the player presses attack is primarily driven by the quality of the animation content." The animation makes the punch feel real to the player with its visual details, such as the arc of the swing and the reactions of characters on the screen.

How Do You Become an Animator?

Education

Students can take classes related to video game animation as early as high school. Any drawing or graphic arts class will help a person develop the artistic skills necessary for this career. Similarly, computer graphics classes—especially those that specialize in digital art or 3-D modeling—also provide a good basis for animation. Computer programming classes would also help a student better understand the overall process of creating a game, which helps develop the ability to communicate with programmers and designers. Additionally, some students might benefit from taking an anatomy class, in which they study the body. Such courses can help animators pay attention to how bodies move and function.

Companies prefer to hire animators who have an associate's or bachelor's degree in computer arts animation, but other majors in artistic or computer science fields are acceptable. Computer arts animation majors take core classes that include animation fundamentals and design principles, 2-D and 3-D animation, advanced modeling, production studio techniques, and life drawing. These classes tend to feature special projects in which students are asked to apply what they have learned. Michale Warren, a student majoring in computer animation at the Ringling College of Art and Design, describes her sophomore year computer animation project. "We had to do a 10 second animation where an original character enters the frame, sits down, and has some motivation to get up and walk off screen," writes Warren on her blog, *Art By Michale Warren*. These kinds of hand-on projects help students develop the skills that animators use in the industry.

Volunteer Work and Internships

While in high school and college, aspiring animators can hone their skills by volunteering to build animations for others. "Enterprising animators can find many local opportunities to provide animation

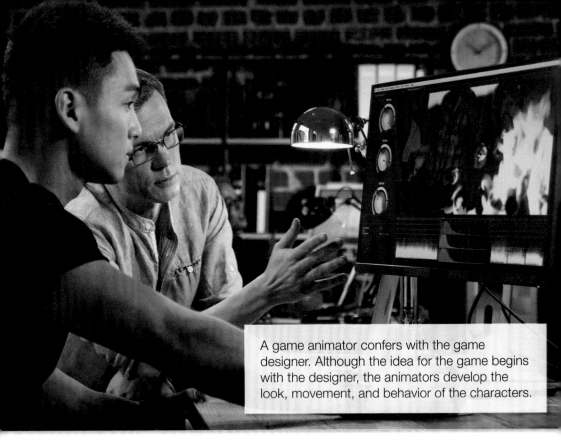

A game animator confers with the game designer. Although the idea for the game begins with the designer, the animators develop the look, movement, and behavior of the characters.

services for schools, nonprofits, small businesses, or community groups, enhancing their websites or contributing animation for an informational short film," states the Study.com article "How to Become an Animator." Those in college or recently graduated should also seek out internship positions in the animator field by searching sites like Internships.com. This is an excellent way to develop on-the-job experience while still working on a degree.

Skills and Personality

Creativity is among the qualities an animator needs to possess. After all, it is the animator's job to take a designer's vision and bring it to life. Animators also need to pay strict attention to detail. They benefit from observing and understanding people and being sensitive to their physical motions, such as how their arms swing while walking or how their face reacts to humor or sadness. Animators use these observations to construct realistic and detailed actions that convey the game's characters and story. "In games where we have realistic animation, often the best you can expect is that nobody notices your animation," explains Barbara Bernad, lead animator of Hitman video games, in an interview on the Art Career Project website, which focuses on art careers. "It means that it looked believable enough so nobody gave it a second thought."

Animators are always working with others, so it is necessary to be a team player. Much animation work is collaborative; during the design phase, an animator meets with designers and game writers to understand the concept for the characters and objects being animated. Upon making their initial creations, animators get feedback from designers to see whether they have met the game's requirements or whether the requirements have changed. Working with programmers is also important, since they are the ones who bring a game's components together in the game engine (the entire game's software framework). Therefore, it is necessary to get along with others, actively listen to their ideas, take feedback and criticism, and effectively communicate.

On the Job

Employers
Many video game studios hire animators on a freelance basis. Freelance workers technically work for themselves and are contracted for work on a per-job basis, rather than serving as a full- or part-time employee of a company. According to the Bureau of Labor Statistics (BLS), 59 percent of multimedia artists and animators (a group that includes video game animators) are self-employed. Those who are employed full time generally work for larger gaming companies such as Nintendo, Rockstar Games, and Sega.

Working Conditions
Animators typically work in an office, either on-site at a company's headquarters or from their own home. They put in long hours at

a desk using various types of computers, monitors, and software programs like Maya. Lionel Gallat, an animator, uses his tools and immediately sees the results. "I just tweak things in Maya, and then click on a button to send everything to Unity and there it is, looking exactly the way the player will see it," Gallat says in an article posted on the Gamasutra website. They also meet regularly with designers, the lead animator, and other animators to collaborate on work. When at their desk, animators use hardware such as a drawing tablet and pen to create character models, and they use software tools to rig and move the characters.

Most animators work regular hours, but if a deadline is approaching, they will typically put in time after hours and on weekends. Because many animators are self-employed and make their own schedule, they might have certain weeks and months in which they are very busy and work more than 40 hours a week, and then they might have weeks or months in which they are between projects and have more flexibility.

Earnings

According to the BLS, in May 2017 the median annual wage for multimedia artists and animators working in computer design was $72,820. The lowest-paid 10 percent of multimedia artists and animators earned less than $39,330, and the highest-paid 10 percent earned more than $123,060. According to *Game Developer* magazine's salary survey, animator salaries depend on one's level of experience. Artists and animators who have less than three years of experience report earning an average salary of $49,481 per year, while those with three to six years of experience average $63,214 per year.

Opportunities for Advancement

Video game animators do not need any specific certification or licensing to work or advance in their career. However, animators who want to advance their careers may consider enrolling in a master's degree program to further develop their skills. For example, earning a master of fine arts in animation and visual effects can help animators become more proficient at using 2-D and 3-D images to tell stories.

Earning a master's degree can also make an animator more eligible for a senior-level position, such as art director. An art director is responsible for the overall design of a gaming project and directs the work of others who develop specific pieces of artwork or create layouts. Another senior-level position is lead animator, who is responsible for the work and progress of other animators on the team.

What Is the Future Outlook for Animators?

The prospect for animators is good, since continued growth is projected throughout the online gaming industry. Consumers increasingly want their video games to feature realistic imagery and movement and for games to be available on numerous platforms, particularly mobile ones. Skilled, multifaceted animators will be needed to meet these demands.

According to the BLS, employment of multimedia artists and animators is projected to grow 8 percent from 2016 to 2026. This is about the average for all occupations, so animator jobs are growing at a similar rate. Despite the expected growth, there will be stiff competition for jobs, since many recent and future graduates are interested in this occupation.

Find Out More

Animation Arena
website: www.animationarena.com

Animation Arena was developed as an online source of information for animators and those interested in animation. This website provides articles about all areas of animation, including 3-D and 2-D, available software, animation schools, and what it is like to work as an animator.

CG Society
website: www.cgsociety.org

The CG Society offers a place for digital artists to connect with each other. The site provides information about the latest in digital art and related educational opportunities. It also provides articles, reels, and workshop information about animation and other digital art.

Society for Animation Studies (SAS)
website: www.animationstudies.org

The SAS was founded in 1987. Through its annual conferences and newsletter, it provides information about animation studies, with papers and articles on animation. The society publishes the journal *Animation Studies* and the blog *Animation Studies 2.0.*, both of which are available on its website.

Women in Animation (WIA)
11400 W. Olympic Blvd. #590
Los Angeles, CA 90064
website: www.womeninanimation.org

The WIA is the only organization dedicated to advancing women in the field of animation. Its goal is to ensure that women have equal opportunity to enjoy the rewards of a career in animation. It provides opportunities for women in the industry to connect with others and publishes biographies of various female animators who work in the industry.

Audio Engineer

Audio engineers fill video games with sound. They use microphones and special software programs to turn everyday sounds into those that can be featured in video games—such as taking the sound of a dropped coin and turning it into a laser blast or turning a dog's bark into the sound of a dragon roaring. Audio engineers both construct new sounds and use sounds from a sound library, which is a compilation of audio files on a software program like Wwise.

The process of finding, generating, and recording sounds begins after a discovery meeting with a game's designers, in which all of the audio requirements for the game are defined. Then audio engineers review the sound effects already in their libraries to determine whether any new sounds need to be created. They may build these sounds in the field, such as by recording the sound of a river, or they may use instruments or everyday objects to create sounds. Adele Kellett, who worked on sound for the game *Harry Potter and the Chamber of Secrets*, describes how she recorded the sound

At a Glance

Audio Engineer

Minimum Educational Requirements
Associate's degree in audio technology or related field preferred

Personal Qualities
Detail oriented, technical, musical

Working Conditions
Indoors, in an office

Pay
About $20,000 to $100,000, depending on experience

Number of Jobs
About 134,300 broadcast and sound technician jobs in 2016

Future Job Outlook
Projected 8 percent growth by 2026

of flushing toilets for the game. "I went to Harrogate Grammar School [in Yorkshire, UK], which is quite an old school, and I knew that when I went there the toilets were very old-fashioned," says Kellett in an interview in the Sound on Sound website. "I had my fingers crossed that they hadn't updated them—and they hadn't. So I looked like a bit of a freak, standing by the toilets flushing them trying to record the sound effects."

Video game audio engineers use a digital audio workstation (DAW), a type of software program, to record and edit sound. One popular program is Pro Tools. After compiling and editing the necessary sounds on the DAW, the audio engineers move the audio files to middleware software like FMOD or Wwise. Middleware allows the engineer to link the audio files to the game engine. Using middleware, the audio engineer can control when certain sounds are triggered in the game. For example, the engineer may set a creaky sound to trigger when a haunted house door is opened. Once an audio engineer has completed his or her work in middleware, the programmers then synthesize the sounds with the game's other components, such as its animation and graphics.

Chase Thompson became a video game audio engineer in 2005 and has worked on best-selling game series like *Halo*, *Fable*, and *Star Wars*. For him, a day at work is never boring. "My favorite part of my job is how varied my work is," Thompson explains in an interview with Jason Bay published on the Game Industry Career Guide website. "One day I might be implementing game music for a new multiplayer mode, the next I might be fixing a bug with one of the vehicle sounds, and the next I might be helping design new and exciting technology with our programming teams."

How Do You Become an Audio Engineer?

Education

One does not need a degree to be an audio engineer, but obtaining one will help a person learn the techniques and technologies required in the field. A bachelor's degree, associate's degree, or even a certificate in audio production from a trade school may give aspiring audio engineers an advantage, since it is a particularly competitive field. Students may also choose to attend a school that offers a relevant degree, such as in sound technology, audio engineering, acoustics, or music recording. For example, the University of Hartford in Connecticut offers students the opportunity to earn a bachelor of science in audio engineering technology, for which they take electronics, acoustics, and music classes. Their program stresses the fundamentals of electronics, music theory, harmony, and sound technology.

At the high school level, students who are interested in obtaining a bachelor's degree in audio engineering can enroll in courses such as physics and precalculus, since higher-level math and science are required for the major. To get experience working with sound systems, high school students can join their school's theater department and work behind the scenes on a production's sound, where they will use microphones, speakers, amplifiers, and mixers.

Volunteer Work and Internships

When hiring for audio engineer positions, many companies look at an applicant's portfolio of projects. One way to gain experience is to volunteer to work with the sound system for a local group such as a church. Kyle Welch is an instructor at Blackbird Academy, which offers six-month programs in audio engineering. "Get behind the board any way you can," Welch says in a blog post on the Blackbird Academy website. "Volunteer to run sound at a friend's rehearsal for their band, volunteer to run sound at a non-profit or church. If you hear about a local event coming up, reach out and see if they have their sound needs in place."

Larger video game producers hire both paid and unpaid interns to do tasks such as set up, configure, and maintain sound equipment and DAWs. Even though some of an intern's responsibilities may be a bit mundane, game companies look for interns who know about sound and audio and who want to learn more.

Skills and Personality

An audio engineer must understand the technology that underlies a game's sound, including the software, middleware, and recording equipment used to create, compile, and edit audio. Additionally, understanding programming is helpful because audio engineers must communicate with programmers about when certain actions will trigger a sound.

Audio engineers must also have a deep understanding of and appreciation for musical concepts, such as harmony, tension, dynamics, scales, modes, and more. This is essential, because in smaller companies the audio engineer may compose or perform music for the game's soundtrack. The audio engineer would need to set up and tune musical instruments, choose and place microphones, run cables, route a signal through audio mixing consoles, and record the music to a DAW.

On the Job

Employers

Audio engineers who have jobs in the online video game industry typically work for development studios, either as salaried employees or as contractors. If an audio engineer works as a contractor or freelancer, it means he or she is hired for a specific project, whereas salaried employees work for a company full time. Working as a contractor or freelancer can offer an audio engineer some flexibility, since he or she is able to take work when offered and choose how many projects to take at a time. However, some do not like not missing out on employer-provided benefits, such as health insurance or paid vacation. Plus there is the stress that comes with not knowing exactly where one's next job will come from. "You will be constantly hunting for your next job," writes video game audio engineer and sound designer, Ted Wennerstrom in the Game Industry Career Guide. "And even when you land one, you will still be looking for the next one."

Working Conditions

Most audio engineers work in a studio that is outfitted with audio equipment. Typically, there is a computer with a DAW and other software and middleware that the engineer uses when editing, compiling, and linking audio files to the game engine. The studio will also have microphones, recorders, instruments, and a mixing console; the larger the company, the more extensive the equipment.

Audio engineers may go on location to record sounds, such as to a field, airport, busy intersection, or windy mountaintop. Chuck Russom, a sound designer who worked on the game series *Call of Duty*, describes how it can be difficult to isolate a desired sound while recording on location. "You are fighting with other sounds in the environment; air traffic, insects/birds, wind, etc.," he explains in an interview with George Spanos posted on the Game Sound Design website.

Audio engineers typically work regular hours but may put in long hours and weekends when a deadline is approaching or when last-minute changes must be made to a game's sounds. For example, during the implementation phase—in which all of a game's components are put together and tested—engineers may discover that the system does not have enough memory to run both the audio and animation in a particular section of the game. At this point the engineer would need to reduce the audio files' size, and quickly.

Earnings

Most video game audio engineers are not hired as full-time employees and thus do not receive a salary. Rather, they work as freelancers or contractors who are hired on a per project basis. According to the Game Industry Career Guide website, video game audio engineers can earn as little as $20,000 annually doing entry-level work, but senior audio engineers in lead positions can earn well over $100,000 per year.

Opportunities for Advancement

Audio engineers can advance their careers by seeking out higher-level jobs such as lead audio, who is in charge of audio for the whole game or a particular section of it. He or she supervises lower-level audio professionals, who may be tasked with setting up equipment, recording, and compiling sounds on the DAW. One very senior position is that of audio engineer director, who is typically in charge of a game's entire audio team. The audio director oversees the creation and implementation of all audio, from music to sound effects to voice. In addition to technical skill and understanding, these jobs require the ability to oversee people, maintain a schedule, and manage a complex budget.

What Is the Future Outlook for Audio Engineers?

The video game industry is growing at a fast pace, and companies compete with each other to earn the most players. One strategy for doing so is to produce games with superior visuals and sound. For this reason, audio engineers are becoming more important as games become more complex and require more intricate and detailed sound.

Audio engineers fall under the category of broadcast and sound engineering technicians, which according to the Bureau of Labor Statistics will experience 8 percent growth by 2026. Despite the numerous opportunities, audio engineering is an extremely competitive field; many talented people are interested in this type of work. "The fact that video games as an industry has . . . overtaken film as a source of entertainment, there are more opportunities to make sound or music for video games than there ever has been," says Will Morton in an interview with GameCareerGuide. Morton formerly worked as a senior audio designer and dialogue supervisor for Rockstar North, which makes the *Grand Theft Auto* video games. While Morton enjoyed his work, he says that making a living as an audio engineer takes hard work and perseverance. "Don't assume that it's easy to get into, or that it's an easy route to earning vast amounts of money quickly," he warns.

Audio Engineering Society (AES)

551 Fifth Ave., Suite 1225
New York, NY 10176
website: www.aes.org

Founded in the United States in 1948, the AES is a professional society devoted exclusively to audio technology. Its website provides links to online articles and publications about the latest audio technology, including video game audio. There are also links to interviews with current audio professionals.

Audio Mentoring Project (AMP)

website: http://audiomentoring.com

The AMP is a group of game audio developers who serve as volunteer mentors to those wanting to enter the field. Its website provides applications for those who want to both mentor and be mentored.

Society for the Study of Sound and Music in Games

website: www.sssmg.org

This international organization is dedicated to understanding how sound and music are used in video games. Its website provides links to different research in video game sound and to events occurring around the nation. It also provides links to other industry-related organizations.

Sound Girls

website: www.soundgirls.org

Sounds Girls is dedicated to supporting women working in audio, including in the video game industry. Its website provides interviews with members, job and internship leads, and articles regarding audio.

Composer

A video game's music is sometimes overlooked amid flashy graphics and a compelling plotline. But video games contain quite a bit of music—there are individual musical themes that accompany specific characters, music that marks different levels and achievements, and a general score or soundtrack that accompanies the entire game. Video game composers write musical scores for video games. They compose music in blocks, small segments of music that engage the player with what is happening at that moment on the screen. A fast-paced musical score may cause a viewer to feel excitement during a chase, while somber music may be appropriate for a scene that takes place on a dark, barren planet. Samantha Foster, a freelance composer for independent video games, says on IndieWatch, "Before I do any track, I ask: What should the emotion, mood, and feel of the track be? I always need this question answered."

To produce music for a video game, composers must first know what sections of the game need music, how long the music should play, and what the mood of the music should be. From there, they

At a Glance

Composer

Minimum Educational Requirements
Bachelor of arts preferred in musical composition or related field

Personal Qualities
Musical, imaginative, self-motivated

Working Conditions
Typically within a studio, either at home or at a company

Pay
Median salary of $50,900 in 2016

Number of Jobs
About 74,800 in 2016

Future Job Outlook
Projected 6 percent growth for all composers through 2026

brainstorm about what type of music to develop and start writing melodies and harmonies for the game's score. Then they use instruments such as flutes, drums, or keyboards to play the music. They record this music with microphones and other equipment that transfer the sound files to recording software, such as Audacity. Composers may also create music directly on a computer using software such as GarageBand and Pro Tools that allow users to create and record music.

After the composer records the music, an audio engineer edits the files and exports them to the game engine. At this point, composers may need to change the music if the mood is not right or the piece does not synchronize with the action. Video game composer Brian Schmidt, who was awarded a Lifetime Achievement Award from the Game Audio Network Guild, recommends that composers be ready to adapt to changes needed in a game. "The music has to be properly integrated into the game, and things can and do go wrong," explains Schmidt on the Game Industry Career Guide website. "Your music may be playing in the wrong place. Or it may conflict with sound effects more than you thought because they added a lot of enemies to a certain section." If so, composers may need to edit or rerecord the music.

Video game studios—particularly the AAA ones, large-scale studios that have high development budgets—regard music as an integral part of any video game. As a result, they provide composers with a lot of resources, such as a budget to hire musicians and the ability to record in high-tech studios. "I think the compositional quality and production levels of music for games is definitely getting better every year," says Jason Graves, a composer for *Tomb Raider* and *Far Cry* games. In an interview with Sean Wilson on Flickering Myth, he says, "I also think the appreciation for game music has risen."

How Do You Become a Composer?

Education
Video game composers do not need a bachelor's degree, but given the intense level of competition for composer jobs, a bachelor's

degree in any music-related field will help. An example of such a degree is a bachelor of arts in music composition. This degree requires students to study tonal harmony, counterpoint (the art of combining melodies in a composition), tonal and nontonal compositional techniques, instrumentation, and orchestration. To prepare for a higher degree in music composition, high school students can take music courses, instrument lessons, and software classes and join bands, orchestras, and other musical groups.

Volunteer Work and Internships

Future composers can build their experience by volunteering in any field that features music, such as by working with a church to produce music for its services. There are also volunteer opportunities within the game industry, and these can sometimes be found by attending game development conventions and offering to help out with their production. "My friend Mark Benis is a young composer who got his first gig working on a game called *Lamplight City* by volunteering at events put on by Playcrafting, an NYC-based organization," says Craig S. Barnes, a video game composer and sound designer, on his personal website. "Volunteering gives you something to do at the event (instead of just standing around), gives you an easy introduction to the event organizer and other volunteers, and people appreciate it."

Skills and Personality

The most critical skill a composer needs is musical ability, and it helps to combine that with a love for video games. Both are necessary to produce music that enhances a game. Video game composer Chris Rickwood, whose credits include games such as *Rising Storm* and *Orcs Must Die!*, believes that passion for both games and music is essential for success in the field. Rickwood explains in the Careers in Music website that aspiring composers need "the ability to write amazing music and convince someone your music is worth paying for. It also would help if you actually played video games and are hip to the video game culture." Tied to that, a video game composer should have technical aptitude — that is, understand how to use recording and editing software

A composer creates an audio sound track for a video game. Before this point, the composer has to find out which sections of the game need music, how long the music should play, and what mood it should convey.

and how to set up hardware such as speakers, audio interfaces, and mixers.

Composers also need to be flexible and remember that they are producing work not for themselves but for a company's product. This means they do not have full creative control over the music they produce. James Hannigan, who composed scores for the *Harry Potter* and *Lord of the Rings* games, thinks it is essential to be easygoing and open to feedback. As he says in Sophia Tong's article "How to Be a Video Game Music Composer—Tips from the Pros" on the GamesRadar+ website, "It's always good to debate the purpose of music, but nobody wants to contend with tension or arrogance when working on a project, so composers have to be flexible enough to adapt. The best composers . . . are the ones who stay open and easy to work with, however established they become."

Employers

Large video game companies can be a great place for composers to find work. Such companies typically develop intricate and detailed games (AAA games) that have higher-quality visuals and audio and have large budgets with which to employ teams of composers. While smaller, independent game developers have less money to work with, composers who work for these developers tend to be given a lot of responsibility, sometimes producing all of the music required for a game by themselves. "Those large-scale, large-budget games ('AAA' games), represent only a very small number professionally created video games each year," states Schmidt on the 2018 Game Music, Sound Design and Virtual Reality Audio Conference website. "For every *Mass Effect* [a popular game], hundreds of small, 2–50 person teams make games for mobile devices, Virtual Reality, PCs and even the major game consoles, Xbox One and PlayStation 4."

Working Conditions

When video game composers are just starting out, most work another full-time job to supplement their income, so they are quite busy. Once they are able to land enough freelance contracts, however, they can feel more confident devoting themselves to composition. They often work a regular schedule, but last-minute changes or fixes can lead some composers to work late nights and weekends to meet a deadline.

Most video game composers are independent contractors who work from their home studios. These studios are typically filled with instruments, a synthesizer, recording equipment, and a computer loaded with mixing and editing software. Most studios include sequencers (devices that can record, edit, and play back music), audio interface equipment, monitors, headphones, microphones, and ideally, a soundproof recording room.

No matter whom they work for, the best composers bring creativity and flexibility to their work. "One of my favorite things is the creative freedom that I get from developers and game companies!" says Karl Magi, a composer of more than twenty-five game soundtracks, in a 2018 article on Spinditty, a website for those interested in music careers. "I feel very fortunate to work with open minded creators. In my opinion, video games are the ultimate artistic medium right now."

Earnings

Video game composers are generally hired on a contract basis, meaning they work on one particular project, as opposed to working for a company full time. According to GameSound-Con, a website for game audio professionals, game composers charge anywhere from $200 to $2,500 per minute of finished music, depending on their experience and the size of the company. Charging $200 per minute of music might break out to as low as $10 per hour of work by the composer, while $2,500 reflects more along the lines of $125 per hour. According to a 2017 GameSoundCon survey, the mean annual salary for audio employees (including sound designers, composers, and audio engineers) was $74,732, and for freelancers was $64,848. Composers can also earn royalties (additional money) after game soundtracks are released.

Opportunities for Advancement

Many video game composers start out as freelance employees and strive to get hired in-house at a video game company. Working in-house typically means that there are more team members with whom to create music and more equipment with which to do it, so composers no longer have to provide their own equipment or do all the work themselves.

Advancing as a composer might mean writing music for bigger-budget video games. With more money at their disposal, composers may be able to hire a team and get access to a larger studio with soundproof recording rooms, live musicians and instruments, and the latest in recording, mixing, and editing hardware and software.

What Is the Future Outlook for Composers?

According the Bureau of Labor Statistics, composer and music director positions should see a growth of 6 percent in the field through 2026; this includes all composers, including those who work for video game companies. Several factors have increased the number of opportunities that exist to make sound or music for video games. One is that the video game industry has overtaken film as a source of entertainment; another is the increase in mobile games being produced, and the fact that the independent game market is growing in general. These factors should ensure that talented video composers will be in high demand for the foreseeable future.

Find Out More

American Society of Composers, Authors, and Publishers (ASCAP)
PO Box 331608-7515
Nashville, TN 37203
website: www.ascap.com

The ASCAP is a nonprofit organization of songwriters, composers, and music publishers, owned and run by its members. It is the world leader in performance royalties, advocacy, and service for music creators. Its website provides information about different industries for these professions, including music publishing in the video game industry.

Game Audio Network Guild
PO Box 1001
San Juan Capistrano, CA 92393
website: www.audiogang.org

The purpose of the Game Audio Network Guild is to build a community of those who work in game audio through an online forum, local chapters, and industry-wide events. Its website includes links to members, industry news, and the guild's own newsletters.

North American Conference on Video Game Music

website: https://vgmconference.weebly.com

The North American Conference on Video Game Music is an annual conference dedicated to music in video games and features scholars in the fields of musicology, music theory, ethnomusicology, media studies, sound studies, composition, and more to discuss all aspects of music in video games. Its website provides links to past conferences and their speakers and topics.

Society of Composers

Box 687
Mineral Wells, TX 76068
website: www.societyofcomposers.org

The Society of Composers is a professional society dedicated to the promotion, performance, understanding, and dissemination of the latest music. Its website includes access to its publication, *SCION*, and a member directory, which includes video game composers. Additionally, the website includes links to student organizations and competitions.

Game Designer

What Does a Game Designer Do?

Without game designers, there would be no games. Game designers conceive of a game's setting, structure, characters, levels, and interface. They also create its goals, rules, and challenges. Some game designers are in charge of an entire game, while others' work may be limited to designing certain characters, levels, or sections of the game. Designers also collaborate with developers, coders, animators, and composers.

G. Kelly Toyama has been designing video games for years. He is best known for his work on *Assassin's Creed: Bloodlines* and *Age of Empires: Mythologies*. As a designer, his job is to lead the push to create the game and ensure it reflects his overall vision. "A little bit of everything," he says of his job description in "How to Become a Video Game Designer" on the Game Industry Career Guide website. "Design is really the go-between with all the disciplines. We have to ride between art, code and production, driving the product forward. It's design's job to try to have a vision of how the game works, what makes it fun, and to be a leader on the team to guide them towards that goal."

At a Glance

Game Designer

Minimum Educational Requirements
Bachelor's degree, preferably in game design or computer science

Personal Qualities
Communicative, creative, motivating

Working Conditions
In an office/studio at a company or at home

Pay
Median salary of $59,951

Number of Jobs
About 73,700 for all multimedia artists and animators, including designers, in 2016

Future Job Outlook
Projected increase of 8 percent through 2026

Abby Friesen, a game designer with Filament Games, also spends much of her day working with others. During the design phase, she develops the designs for the game—from its look to its rules. Once a game is in production, she oversees the work to ensure that all areas, such as the animation, audio, and story, are meeting the design requirements, and she provides feedback to teams if changes are required. "Designers come up with game pitches, write game design documents (and pretty much everything else that requires writing), create storyboards, make levels, balance the games, lead teams, create narrative and dialog, write up tasks for all the features in the game, and make lots and lots of spreadsheets," Friesen explains in a 2015 interview with Kat Shanahan on the Filament Games website. "Most of my day is spent making sure everything is implemented in the game correctly and making content for it if needed (such as level design)."

Paolo Malabuyo, a lead design program manager with Xbox and Microsoft, says that ultimately, the joy of working in game design is seeing how much people enjoy the results. "In the end, what you're responsible for as a game designer is whether a game is fun or not," Malabuyo says in an interview published on All Art Schools, an online directory of art schools and related resources. "When you listen to a group of people who just played a fun multiplayer game together, it sounds as if they are telling the story of something they just did in reality," he notes.

How Do You Become a Game Designer?

Education

Most companies prefer to hire designers who have a bachelor's degree in computer science, game design, computer engineering, or a related degree. Those who major in game design can take very specialized courses. For example, those who want to design games for Android smartphones will concentrate on the programming language Java and the Android OS. Developing games for the Apple iOS operating system will require students to take courses on Objective-C. Students who aspire to become video game designers should also take courses on theories of animation, computer science and programming, and various programing languages and coding. Taking art courses is also beneficial.

While in school, students should consider joining game development clubs or organizations, such as the International Game Developers Association. Doing so can help future game designers make connections in the industry and create projects with others interested in these subjects. Most colleges have coding and art clubs in which students can make prototypes of games and visuals and use these to develop a portfolio of projects, such as mini games and other designs. This work can be shown to prospective employers when applying for a job.

Volunteer Work and Internships

Game design internships offer those interested in this field a window into what game design is like and the chance to develop contacts. Depending on the studio, internships may be paid or unpaid and are typically available in the summer or as a first job after graduation. An article on the Chron website titled "Jobs That Will Give Experience in the Video Game Industry" explains that "many companies offer summer and fall internships where you will do menial things such as food delivery, bug testing, and memo drafting. Interning at a game company, however, is a foot in the door, and it provides invaluable experience."

One of the best ways to volunteer is to find nearby gaming events or conventions and ask whether they need help setting up booths and equipment or with other tasks. Most will be glad for the help, and doing so offers volunteers an inside look at how video game events are run, the latest industry developments, and who the key players are in the industry. Examples of such conventions include the Game Developers Conference, the Game On Expo, and the Electronic Entertainment Expo.

Skills and Personality

Game designers need to be imaginative. When it comes down to it, their main job is to get a potential player to put down everything else and play their game. To do this, the game must have a

The game designer makes sure that the animation, story, and audio all come together to meet the design goals. To do this, game designers frequently meet with others who are working on the project.

unique and intriguing plot, look, sound, and style. John Newcomer is a designer who started working in the game industry during its infancy in the 1980s. Newcomer designed the arcade game *Joust*, which is now a cultural icon, and in the time since has held design and director positions at game studios. "To make a game you have to realize that you're competing for a customer's free time doing anything entertaining," Newcomer explains in an article published on the Pluralsight website. "I have to make the game more enticing than watching a movie or listening to music."

Game designers must possess certain technical skills so they can work with animators, graphic artists, programmers, and others who bring a game to life. Specifically, they need to understand 2-D and 3-D graphics and animation packages, such as Autodesk 3ds Max, NUKE, or Maya. They should also be familiar with the various game platforms, such as tablets, handheld devices, consoles, and PCs, and how to design specifically for these platforms. Game designers use other tools, such as Adobe Creative Suite for video and image editing; C++, Python, and C# for object-oriented programming; and Visual Studio and Unity for coding and game development.

Motivating others is a big part of the job; the designer provides the vision for the game but must work with a team to ensure it is achieved. "If you find yourself at a point where you are dictating or mandating, then you have lost the thread of the design process," explains Toyama. "You are the visionary, but that means gathering together the vision of the team, not forcing your own vision down their throats."

Game designers also need to be good communicators and listeners. They need to effectively communicate their vision and plans and listen to feedback throughout the process. Tim Lang, a game designer at Spin Master Studios, says, in a 2018 article published on Game Career Guide, that a "huge portion of being a game designer is communicating your ideas and designs to other members of the development team." As development teams continue to get larger and larger, the importance of communication becomes greater and greater.

On the Job

Employers

Game designers typically work for game development companies, software publishers, and game studios, which can range from small independent shops to large corporations. According to the Entertainment Software Association, in 2017 there were 2,457 game companies of varying sizes within the United States. The states with the most game companies were California, Texas, and Washington. Game designers who work at big companies typically work with other designers on a team that is overseen by a lead designer. Designers who work for smaller, independent companies often have more responsibility for the overall design, since there may be just a few designers on the project.

Working Conditions

Video game designers typically work in an office or studio with others on their team. Their workplaces may be a cubicle, a single office, or an open area with workstations throughout. The most well-known gaming companies, like EA in San Francisco, offer amenities like coffee shops, game rooms, and gyms for employees to enjoy on breaks. Most game companies have a casual business environment in which people do not need to dress formally for work. Although the atmosphere is informal, most companies demand a high level of performance, both in work quality and meeting deadlines.

Most designers work a regular schedule but put in overtime to meet deadlines or make last-minute changes. Even if they are not on a deadline, many designers are so passionate about their work that they have a hard time putting it aside. "I bet if I counted an 'easy' week for me [it] would be a 60 hour week," says Steve Bowler, a game designer at Phosphor Studios, in a 2015 article on Lifehacker. "Most weeks I bet I do 80 hours at a minimum. I'm frequently stealing hours on the weekend to work on my laptop polishing things in the game."

Earnings

Video game designers who are full-time employees typically earn a regular salary. According to salary data from PayScale, a company that analyzes compensation, the median wage for a video game designer in 2018 was $59,951, with half making more and half making less. The lowest-paid 10 percent of game designers made under $36,302, and the highest-paid 10 percent earned over $99,140. A game designer's salary is influenced by both where he or she works and any special skills he or she possesses. Where one lives can make a difference, too: Game designers in San Francisco reported earning a median wage of $70,246, while those in Seattle earned $64,479. With experience, designers typically achieve significant wage increases and may be promoted to a senior game designer role.

Opportunities for Advancement

Game designers can advance to become a senior game designer or lead designer. On-the-job experience and comfort working with others are necessary to advance in this field. In these positions, game designers lead other designers. The lead game designer takes concepts offered by all the game designers in brainstorming sessions and creates clear ideas for the game's locations, characters, rules, story, objects, interface, and modes. A lead designer then works closely with artists and programmers to achieve these elements.

After working as a lead designer, one might advance to the position of creative director. Creative directors are responsible for a product's overall vision, which includes how the game is played, as well as its visual style, overall story, audio, animation, and marketing materials. Often, the creative director comes up with a game's entire concept.

What Is the Future Outlook for Game Designers?

The Bureau of Labor Statistics includes video game designers in the category of animators and multimedia artists. This category is projected to experience 8 percent growth through 2026, increasing the number of jobs by sixty-two hundred. This growth is likely due to growing interest in online video games, which are increasingly easier to access with smartphones, tablets, and other mobile devices.

Find Out More

Academy of Interactive Arts & Sciences

3183 Wilshire Blvd., Suite 196 F13
Los Angeles, CA 90010
website: www.interactive.org

This not-for-profit organization is dedicated to the advancement and recognition of the interactive arts. It has more than thirty thousand members. Its website includes interviews with many within the gaming industry, a podcast featuring interviews with game makers, and industry awards for game makers.

Entertainment Software Association
601 Massachusetts Ave. NW, Suite 300
Washington, DC 20001
website: www.theesa.com

The Entertainment Software Association is dedicated to serving the business and public affairs needs of companies that publish computer and video games for video game consoles, handheld devices, personal computers, and the Internet. Its website includes game industry statistics, articles about the game industry, and a newsletter.

Game Designing
website: www.gamedesigning.org

This website was created to help aspiring game designers learn how to become professional. It includes articles about game design, information about game design college programs, and links to software tools such as Unity.

International Game Developers Association (IGDA)
50 Eglinton Ave. E., Suite 402
Toronto, ON M4P 1E8
website: www.igda.org

The IGDA is a nonprofit professional association that brings together people from all fields of game development—from programmers and producers to writers and artists. Its website provides articles on game industry news, links to different chapters, and a career search engine.

Game Producer

What Does a Game Producer Do?

Game producers hold one of the highest positions in a game's production and have the responsibility of running the entire project from conception to implementation. The game producer is ultimately responsible for producing a quality game on schedule. A game producer first assembles and manages a team of software engineers, programmers, writers, animators, audio engineers, designers, and artists. He or she creates the game production schedule and uses it to track tasks and ensure the design is implemented on time. A game producer also works with the company's public relations department to promote and sell the game. The producer is the link between all teams working to develop the game. As such, it is his or her responsibility to facilitate communication between key areas, such as game design, programming, and testing.

Who a producer interacts with during the day depends on the size of the company. In smaller, independent studios, a game producer may directly interact with programming and creative staff; he or she may even jump in and code a portion of the game or test it. At larger gaming companies, the producer generally oversees the leads of different departments, such as programming and design, who in turn provide him or her with status updates from their departments.

Frank Rogan is a senior video game producer who has worked on many game titles, including *Enter the Matrix*, *Gears & Guts*, and the *Total Annihilation* series. He explains that a game producer essentially owns the entire project, from vision to production. His day is filled with many different tasks that include both long-term planning and troubleshooting daily issues. "At any given time, a producer could be working with designers to break down their ideas into specific tasks, working through code problems with engineers, or making sure that artistic feedback is complete and actionable," Rogan says in an interview with Jason Bay on the Game Industry Career Guide website. "Or, you could just have your head buried in a spreadsheet." No matter what he is doing, Rogan finds his days exciting because they are filled with different tasks such as thinking creatively, interacting with people, and creating games people love.

How Do You Become a Game Producer?

Education

A bachelor's degree in game design, digital media, or computer science would help an aspiring producer learn the game-making process. Because game producers oversee an entire project, it is essential to understand how to use 2-D and 3-D animation packages, programming languages such as Java, Visual Basic, and C++, and audio software like Wwise and Audacity. Courses in statistics, business management, finance, and accounting are also useful because producers are often in charge of the budget and schedule for the game production.

Rogan recommends that high school and college students teach themselves many of the requisite skills by making their own games. "Make something. Anything," Rogan suggests. "You want to get into games? Show me the little Flash game you made and put on your Web site. I kid you not, making your own Flash game will be worth thousands of dollars of classes at any university." He and others in the industry recommend that aspiring video game producers set up a website to showcase their projects.

Because being a producer requires leadership, aspiring game producers should take on leadership roles in clubs or jobs in which they are in charge of projects and other people. Ellen Beeman, an executive game producer with more than fifteen years of experience at companies such as Microsoft and Disney, explains how she first learned skills needed to lead others. "In college, I worked part-time at a music studio as a producer," she says in the article "Ask the Experts: How to Become a Producer," published on Gamasutra. "It never amounted to much, but that managerial experience helped me get my first project director job at Sierra [a game publisher]. Any professional experience, even not related to the game industry, is great. It all helps."

Volunteer Work and Internships

Holding any type of internship in the game industry will help put a person on a path to becoming a producer. Because a producer has to know all the key areas of game building, any internship experience, such as serving as a tester or a programmer, will prove useful. One place to look for internships is on the International Game Developers Association website.

Volunteering is another way to get one's foot in the door. Volunteering at a gaming company or convention can offer an inside look at the latest games and trends and a chance to hear and meet people who work in the industry. Consider the IndieCade, an independent game convention held in Los Angeles, New York City, and Paris. People can apply for volunteer positions to help demonstrate games, set up exhibitions, and help attendees find their way around the convention. Volunteers are allowed to attend the events when they are not working.

Skills and Personality

A video game producer has to be detail oriented or the game will not be completed accurately or on time. He or she needs to ensure that all the different teams complete their tasks on time and work together to meet all requirements. En Masse Entertainment video producer Chris Hager, in an interview with Sebastian Haley published on the VentureBeat website, says, "It's this love of intricacy and detail, along with an appreciation for a well-made product, that makes me love being a video game producer."

Even though game producers are not programmers, they must be able to communicate with programmers and understand their work. Therefore, game producers need to broadly understand each component of game development. In larger companies, this is necessary so that the producer is able to communicate effectively with the leads of the different game areas. At smaller companies, producers may even need to step in and help with different aspects of the job, including coding, animation, and audio.

Game producers need to be decisive people, since they are in charge of making many of the most important decisions about a game's genesis. If problems arise, the producer must be able to tell others what to do. He or she must be able to communicate well so that others understand what is expected of them, and the producer must also listen well to clearly understand the status of each team working on the project.

On the Job

Employers

Most producers work for gaming studios, which can range from small, independent start-ups to large-scale corporate entities. Companies that hire producers are looking for people who have a lot of experience in the industry. The major companies tend to be located in metropolitan areas such as San Francisco, Dallas, and Philadelphia.

Producers may also start their own companies and produce their own games. Independent studios have popped up across the United States to meet the demand of the ever-expanding game market. Depending on how much money a producer has to start the company and hire workers, he or she may have to adopt many or all of the development roles.

Sam Browne first worked as an intern at a big-name studio, TT Games, and then decided to start his own studio, Three Knots, with a partner and produce games. "Anyone starting up an indie studio should see what's what in a big studio, especially how they operate and what you can take from that system," Brown recommends in an interview published on the Red Bull website.

Working Conditions

Although they typically have their own office, producers rarely sit and work alone—much of their day involves being around people. Meeting with an animator to help solve a problem with movement, talking to a programmer about a realistic time to complete a section of code, and encouraging a writer who is stuck on a story line could all be part of a producer's day. "I love working with people, I love helping people achieve their best work, to make them happy to come to work every day, and every day I get to do that," says Ryan Treadwell, a producer at the game studio Certain Affinity, in an article published on the game industry site Kotaku. "It is the coolest thing in the whole world. I get to work with absolute geniuses."

Video game producers may be called to work longer hours or over weekends to ensure the game is on track. Rogan, a senior video game producer, says, "If you're looking for a position where you can punch a clock, do your work and go home, production is not for you. Every day is 'Anything Can Happen Day.'" For this reason, the job can be stressful. However, this is also what is exciting about the job. Many game producers thrive on the challenge of completing a high-quality project that players will love.

Earnings

According to PayScale, a video game producer earns an average salary of $72,798 per year. PayScale found that an entry-level video game producer with less than five years of experience could expect to earn about $61,000, which includes a bonus and overtime pay. A video game producer who is midcareer and has a lot of experience can expect to earn around $75,000. A very experienced video game producer can earn upward of $145,000.

Opportunities for Advancement

Typically, game producers come up in the industry, having started as testers, designers, and/or programmers. They might then move into an associate producer job at a mid- or large-scale company and be in charge of a portion of the game, or they might produce the entire game at a small company. After getting experience as an associate producer, they might move into a lead producer, executive producer, or senior producer position. These jobs are typically available at big video game publishers like Sony and Electronic Arts, as opposed to independent development companies.

For years, Heather Hazen was the executive producer of *Bejeweled*, a popular online game that has been reinvented many times over the past decade. Hazen talks about how her job required her to interface with many different teams and work on various aspects of the game. She explains that part of her job was to bring together teams working on different platforms of *Bejeweled* to determine the best way to standardize the game across all different platforms. "We had this little social studio that was thinking about Facebook and a mobile studio that was thinking about moving towards smartphones and they weren't really having conversations with one another," Hazen explains on Complex, a pop culture website. "My big job was to unify the teams and think of a way that we could build a *Bejeweled Blitz* ecosystem that was sustainable across multiple platforms."

What Is the Future Outlook for Game Producers?

The Entertainment Software Association reports that 65 percent of American households play video games. The 2017 *Year in Review Report* by SuperData Research shows that mobile games generated $59.2 billion that year, followed by PCs (at $33 billion) and consoles (at $8.3 billion). Such growth is expected to continue. This increasing demand for challenging and entertaining games, and the increasing use of mobile phones and tablets, indicates that game producer positions will enjoy steady growth. According to Vault.com, employment in this job should grow at a faster-than-average rate over the next decade.

Find Out More

Game Producer's Guide to the Galaxy
website: www.gameproducersguide.com

This website provides information on video game production, design tools, and the latest game ideas in the industry, all of which producers need to know. It is run by a veteran of the game industry and aims to provide those in the industry with advice and best practices.

Games Industry Biz
website: www.gamesindustry.biz

This website offers articles on the latest news in the games industry—technology, game, and business related, all of which relate to the work of a producer. The site also hosts a games industry career search engine and has links to the latest industry events, such as expos.

Pocket Gamer
website: www.pocketgamer.biz

This site provides the latest articles, interviews, information, and news regarding mobile games. It also links to upcoming expos on mobile gaming, which game designers and producers attend. The site also has a search engine for finding careers in the gaming industry.

VentureBeat
website: https://venturebeat.com

This website is a source for news and events for developers, enthusiasts, and business leaders. It provides articles on the latest technologies, designs, and business happenings in the gaming industry. Visitors can also subscribe to a newsletter.

Programmer

What Does a Programmer Do?

Video game programmers use language, or code, that tells computers what to do. Such instructions pertain to everything from a video game's rules to its graphics. A game programmer's main task is to take the concepts created by a game's artists and designers and translate these into computer platforms using coding languages such as C++.

Video games often require several different types of programming. Artificial intelligence (AI) programmers make a game lifelike, because their job is to make the game react to a player's moves. AI programmers code how nonplayer characters react to a player's moves. Network programmers' code allows gamers to interact with one another online. User interface programmers write code that determines how the user can interact with the game, including starting, pausing, and saving games. In larger studios a programmer is usually assigned to one of these areas, whereas in a smaller company the programmer may be expected to program several areas of the game.

Programmers receive requirements and deadlines from a game's designers or its lead programmers. Then they begin to code. They may be coding from scratch, creating everything needed using source code such as C#. However, many will work in a game engine such as Unity, which is a suite of development tools that have reusable software components such as graphics, sound, and AI functions. Programmers can use code to modify, add, and delete what is in the engine but do not need to code common functions that are used in most games. The game engine allows programmers to avoid reinventing the wheel and focus on adding or creating functionality unique to their game.

Programmers regularly meet with designers to make sure they understand the artistic concepts and to receive feedback on their work. Programmers also fix errors, or bugs, that inevitably crop up in their code, and they revise the code as needed. "A game programmer needs to understand the more ephemeral concepts that artists and designers come up with, and translate them into concrete systems in code," Dan Posluns says on Game Industry Career Guide. Posluns has worked as a programmer on *The Sims* and *LEGO Star Wars* games. He says,

> I'm usually the only one who really understands how those systems work. I need to completely simulate the ideas of those artists and designers, and at the same time consider the runtime performance costs.

How Do You Become a Programmer?

Education

High school students who hope to become video game programmers should take higher-level math classes, such as precalculus and calculus, and any type of computer science classes. When in college, students should earn a bachelor's degree in computer science, software engineering, or a related field. In most of these majors, students take core classes in mathematics, computer science, and data analysis. In their junior and senior years, students take more specific topics, such as advanced programming. Some programs require students to take lab courses in which they develop their own software or game. Most students are required to learn computer languages like C+, C++, and Java.

Professional programmers suggest that students program games on their own time, outside of class. "I worked on my own indie games very early on, whether plunking away on my Apple IIc or on a TI-85 calculator," says Posluns. "I think that's how a lot of game programmers get started: by working on their own little pet projects." Some online software programs, such as Unity, are free to download, and students can use them to practice making games.

Certification and Licensing

Although it is not required, video game programmers may choose to become certified by the Institute for Certification of Computing Professionals. This is not a certification specific to video game programming but pertains to programming in general. The institute offers the Certified Computing Professional credential to people who earn a bachelor's degree, work full time for two years in programming, and pass three certification exams with a 70 percent or higher score. The certification exams consist of a core exam and two specialty exams, such as object-oriented analysis and design, procedural programming, and systems programming. Being certified may give job applicants an edge when applying for programming work.

Volunteer Work and Internships

As a student or a new graduate, getting an internship in the video game industry is a solid way to get into the business. However, internships are highly coveted experiences, and there is a lot of competition for them among aspiring programmers. Companies like Nintendo and Microsoft offer internships and tend to choose those with technical knowledge of C++ and other programming languages such as Python.

Both high school and college students can get programming experience by volunteering with local groups that are working to

The job of the programmer is to create and input the coding that enables the video game to run. Their work also shapes the quality of user interaction with the game.

get students interested in computer science. One such group is Code for Fun, a San Francisco–based organization that runs programs that expose students to computer science at an early age; people age sixteen and older can apply to volunteer. Other organizations such as Code.org host an Hour of Code, an event at which volunteers teach coding to students for one hour.

Skills and Personality

Those who program video games must pay strict attention to very tiny details; one mistake in a single line of code can cause problems in a game's performance. James Gale, who has programmed games for more than ten years, says that his early coding work would have been much better had he gone over each line carefully. "I think my code would have improved a lot faster if I took the time to understand every line I had in my programs," he says in a 2015 interview on AIE, a website about game education, "even if it meant spending more time writing smaller, much more boring programs before I got to write fully fledged games."

Good programmers also enjoy learning and continually seek out opportunities to expand their skills, learn new programs, and stay on top of what's going on in the industry. Different projects may require a programmer to code in different languages and use a specified game engine, such as Unreal Engine or Unity. Game engines are constantly evolving with new functionality. Programmers need to evolve with the technology and learn as they go.

Programmers also need to be passionate about their work. They should love to build programs and, when they encounter a problem or error, should feel driven to find out how to fix it. Programmers are natural problem solvers who are driven by their love of error-free work.

Finally, video game programmers must be highly logical. "Once you understand computers follow basic rules of logic in order to do their job, you will see there is always an answer to a problem," states the website Learn to Code with Me. "You just have to use logic to figure it out."

On the Job

Employers

Thousands of game companies have opened across the United States in the past three decades, and these have generally clustered in metropolitan areas. Therefore, a programmer is more likely to find a job in a city like Los Angeles or New York. Some gaming studios are small independent companies that hire small teams, while others are huge companies like Nintendo that have locations around the world. All game companies need programmers, so opportunities abound at companies of all sizes.

Working Conditions

Some think that programmers just sit at a desk, typing on a computer all day. In actuality, a programmer's work environment varies per job. Some companies may provide cubicles or private offices for their programmers to help them code without distraction. Other companies prefer programmers to work in one large, open room to encourage them to interact with each other. Open offices often provide couches, scattered tables, and breakout areas without walls.

Salaried programmers generally work regular forty-hour weeks, with weekends off. Due to the nature of the business, with deadlines and unexpected changes or errors to fix, programmers will likely work some overtime and weekends. "While the amount of crunch varies widely from company to company, it's pretty rare to find a studio that doesn't occasionally go through a crunch of some kind," says Posluns. "It can be hard to strike a proper work-life balance in games, so it's important to take responsibility for your own health and well-being."

Earnings

According to the Bureau of Labor Statistics (BLS), in 2017 the median salary for computer programmers, which includes video game programmers, was $84,240. According to PayScale, the average salary for a video game programmer is $65,244 per year; a senior game programmer earns $99,749. PayScale's research shows that the highest-paid programmers are those who have skills in C++, past experience programming for games, and skills with object-oriented programming.

Opportunities for Advancement

After putting in many years working on teams, experienced programmers can advance to become a lead programmer. A lead programmer translates a game's design into technical requirements and then assigns and distributes tasks to the programming team. For example, the lead programmer may divide the requirements into areas such as programming the game logic, programming the user interface actions, and coding the links between animations to user action. He or she ensures all components are being programmed on schedule and tracks any bugs or errors found during testing. Gale says a video game programmer can expect to be a team lead after about five years in the industry. In an interview on AIE, he says that being a team lead "meant doing things like delegating tasks, helping other coders when they ran into problems, discussing the viability of features with producers, designers and artists and generally being responsible for the project moving forward."

The most sought-after game programmers are those who program specifically for PCs, consoles, cell phones, or online environments or who work in a particular aspect of game development, such as special effects, artificial intelligence, or network performance. "At the junior- to mid-level, people are pretty fluid between [platforms]," says Phil Steinmeyer, founder of New Crayon Games. In an article titled "Career Spotlight: Game Programmer" published on the website Monster, he says, "At the senior level, part of what you're bringing to the table is expertise on a particular platform."

What Is the Future Outlook for Programmers?

According to the BLS, the employment of all computer programmers is projected to decline 7 percent in the United States from 2016 to 2026. This is partly due to the fact that computer programming can be done from anywhere in the world, and some US-based companies may choose to hire programmers in countries where employees are typically paid lower salaries than their American counterparts. However, some project a brighter future for programmers in the video game industry. Scott Miller, chief executive officer of the game development studio 3D Realms, sees positive signs for programmers in the field. "This industry is still growing and needs fresh new talent by the truckloads," says Miller in "Career Spotlight: Game Programmer" on Monster. "If you've got talent and know how to package it and yourself, you're a shoo-in."

Find Out More

Dream.In.Code
website: www.dreamincode.net

Dream.In.Code is an online community for programmers and web developers. As of September 2018, there were 661,258 registered members. Members have free access to programming tutorials, code snippets, forum topics, and more, including question and answer sections.

GameDev.net
website: www.gamedev.net

GameDev.net is a game development community platform where people can connect with others in the game programming and development industry. On this site, they can find articles and links to information about game programming and search for job opportunities. The site publishes articles and tutorials on all different areas of the video game industry, including programming.

Unity
30 Third St.
San Francisco, CA 94103
website: www.unity3d.com

Unity game engine software tools allow game programmers and developers to create half of the world's games. Its website offers a free download of Unity and a tutorial on how to use it. The site also hosts numerous communities and forums where users can discuss various aspects of Unity.

Unreal Engine
Epic Games
620 Crossroads Blvd.
Cary, NC 27518
website: www.unrealengine.com

Unreal Engine is a complete suite of development tools that can be used to design and develop video games. People can download Unreal Engine 4 to practice creating games. Its website includes tutorials, documentation, and links to articles about Unreal Engine, games that use it, and its features.

Tester

What Does a Tester Do?

A video game tester's job is to play a game and look for flaws, such as glitches within the game, broken applications, or non-functioning visual effects. Testers probe all aspects of a game trying to find discrepancies or areas that perform slowly. The goal is to ensure that games meet certain standards and requirements and to fix any issues before the game is rolled out to the public. Game-testing work is also known as quality control inspection or quality assurance.

Video game testers are typically assigned a specific part of a game, such as a fight scene between the player and a villain, and given a description of what is supposed to happen. Testers then perform several different functions, such as hitting the opponent or running away, as they search for bugs. "While playing *Terraria* (an open-world, endless game like *Minecraft*), our team of eight to ten guys used to sit together," explains Mitch, a former game tester, in an article published by Mashable. "Every person had to focus on one task: One had to dig iron only for days, the other had to dig gold, and likewise every guy had to focus on single tasks and test for days just to check for any issues."

At a Glance

Tester

Minimum Educational Requirements
None required; high school degree preferred

Personal Qualities
Meticulous, focused, patient

Working Conditions
Indoors, in an office at a game studio or at home

Pay
Average salary of $31,000

Number of Jobs
About 287,000 in 2016

Future Job Outlook
Projected 5 percent to 9 percent growth through 2026

Testers specifically check to see whether video games perform according to the designer's specifications and user's requirements. They also test the game's network performance, installation, and configuration. After they test these and other aspects of a game, testers write a report on their findings and send the game back to the programmers for revisions and corrections. The revised version of the game, known as a new game build, will then go back to the tester, and this process continues until all problems are fixed.

Spending one's day playing video games might sound ideal to some people, but professional video game testers admit that their workdays can get monotonous. The same aspect of a game often has to be tested over and over. For example, a tester might have to spend all day slamming into every wall in the latest *Call of Duty* to see if the wall stays in place. Or a fighting game may have twenty different characters with twenty levels, and the tester will need to play every character against every other character on every single level.

However, the benefits include getting to work on games that are interesting and being a part of a team that produces a high-quality final product. Successful testers find it exciting and challenging to test every little detail of a game, and they enjoy getting to be a part of the process. "My favorite part of the job was the ability to see how new games were made, everything from the planning process to the early stage of development to the final finished product," says Bayaar Lo-Borjiged, a former video game tester, in a 2017 article published on the Mental Floss website.

How Do You Become a Tester?

Education

Testing is an entry-level job in the game industry, so a degree is not typically required. However, a bachelor's degree will help those looking to move up in the quality assurance field or to earn higher pay have a better chance of doing so. Recommended degrees include those related to information systems, game design, or software development.

Understanding video games and learning about all aspects of them are the key to getting the experience needed to be a tester. Video game producer Aaron Roseman hires testers for his studio, Treyarch. In an interview on the website Careers Out There, he describes a tester's job as follows: "It's their job to break the game, crash the game, see what sort of weird graphical issues they can [cause to] occur, [make] sure that the lighting looks well, the characters don't run into walls, the game doesn't crash, that everything sounds well."

Industry experts like Roseman suggest that those who want to test video games should play several types of games, such as shooting games (which feature weapons), sports games, survival games (such as *Fortnite*), and puzzle games like *Words with Friends*. Instead of trying to win a game, students should focus on observing all the different details—tiny visual details, sounds, and the reactions of other characters or the environment to a player's actions. Students should also take note of how fast or slowly the game performs during different sections. For example, when playing in *Minecraft*, an aspiring tester could practice doing the same tasks, such as mining, jumping, and sprinting, as different skins (characters) to observe how the audio and visuals are different for each skin.

Certification and Licensing

No certification or licensing is required to be a tester. However, the Quality Assurance Institute offers certification for a software quality analyst. To earn this certification, one must pass an exam and fulfill other requirements, such as having a bachelor's degree from an accredited university and two years' experience working in the information services field or a two-year degree from an accredited university and four years' experience. This certification may help a tester who is looking to rise to the level of lead tester or to test a major game made by a large company.

Volunteer Work and Internships

Volunteering can be one path for those interested in breaking into video game testing. Volunteers might get in touch with an indie studio and offer to test their games free of charge. Indie studios are typically small—sometimes they consist of just one or two employees—and thus cannot usually afford to pay a tester. Despite this, there is still work to be done. Offering to be a beta tester—that is, someone who tests a game when it is completed as opposed to testing the game throughout production—and testing a game for free "can be a good way for you to learn game testing *and* put some testing experience on your resume," writes Jason Bay in "How to Become a Video Game Tester (FAQ)" on Game Industry Career Guide.

Skills and Personality

Video game testers need to be very detail-oriented people. They must enjoy focusing on the micro details—such as having a character walk through a forest and observe every tree to see if the trees are missing any leaves or are the correct color—as they do their work. They also need to have patience; they must often test the same areas of a game over and over again, continuously looking for errors, mistakes, and other out-of-place details.

Testers need to be able to keep their focus on the same project for a long time, even months or years, because most modern PC or console games take one to three years to complete. Testing continues after bugs and errors are found and fixed by programmers. "You need to have a good attention span, and not get bored of a game even after you've been testing it for a long time," writes Bay. "And I mean, for a looooooong time—modern, triple-A games can take up to five years of development and testing before they're released to the public."

Finally, video game testers must be trustworthy and discreet. "Being a game tester, by definition, means working on a game that is not publicly available," says former video game tester Mark Kaelin in a 2017 article published in TechRepublic. "In some cases, the game may even be a closely held secret. Successful game tester candidates must demonstrate the ability to keep a secret and honor non-disclosure agreements."

On the Job

Employers

Most game-testing jobs are located in the same cities where the large game studios are headquartered. Although the United States has the most gaming studios of any country, England, Canada, and Japan also are home to many game companies. Cities like Seattle, Montreal, Tokyo, and London offer several opportunities. "You may be able to find testing jobs in smaller towns and cities," suggests Bay on Game Industry Career Guide. "But if you're positive that you want to break into the game industry then you'll have the best chances of finding work if you can move to one of the major cities for game development."

Working Conditions

Testers generally do much of their work alone, especially while they are exploring the game builds, revised versions of the game that are updated as corrections are made. However, they often need to interact with designers (to better understand a game's requirements) and programmers (to provide reports about what they found during their tests). They also may interact with other testers who are working on different aspects of the game.

Testers generally work in a quiet area, whether at home or in an office, because they need to concentrate on the game and its details. Often, they wear headphones compatible with the mobile device or computer so that they can zero in on the game's sounds. The ability to stay focused is important because a game's details are crucial to its success. For example, if a tester works on a section of a game for several hours and it crashes, he or she must be able to recall the exact last few moves or keystrokes entered and record this in the bug log.

Earnings

According to the job search engine Indeed, the average salary for a video game tester was $39,637 per year in 2018. This was based on information the site received from employees, users,

A video game tester is involved in quality control. Testers search for programming glitches and other problems that would affect the user experience.

and past and present job advertisements in the previous thirty-six months. Similarly, PayScale reports that the average video game tester earns $31,000 per year in the United States. Pay variations are based on location, a company's size, and how many years of experience a tester has.

Opportunities for Advancement

Game tester positions are considered entry level in the industry. Those who want to stay in testing might aim to be promoted to a lead or manager position. In addition to demonstrating their ability to perform quality tests, those who want to advance in this area need to be able to direct others.

However, many see the next step for a tester as moving over to a different area of the game industry, such as programming or producing. "The thing I dislike most is that it's incredibly hard to move one's career forward," says Lo-Borjiged of game testing. "To work your way out of testing you really, really have to stand out, and that is hard given how many other testers there can be from company to company." Lo-Borjiged knows this from firsthand experience—he worked his way up from being a game tester to working on user interface design and eventually became chief executive officer of Skull Fire Games.

What Is the Future Outlook for Testers?

The demand for video game testers is closely related to the demand for video games themselves, which is on an upward trend. Additionally, as programming increasingly features the latest technology—such as virtual reality—there will be a greater need for testers because the games will have more details. In 2016 O*NET Resource Center reported that 287,000 people worked in software quality assurance, which includes video game testers. O*NET projects a growth of 5 percent to 9 percent in this area through 2026.

Find Out More

Quality Assurance Institute (QAI)
5728 Major Blvd., Suite 602
Orlando, FL 32819
website: www.qaiusa.com

The QAI provides instructor-led trainings, career programs, exam preparatory training, and certification for both individuals and organizations in quality assurance. Its website includes webinars on different quality assurance topics, including software testing, and information on its software testing certifications.

Software Test Professionals
4746 Desert Candle Dr.
Pueblo, CO 81001
website: www.softwaretestpro.com

Software Test Professionals is an online community that provides software testing information and networking. Its website offers white papers, news, articles, conferences, events, and other information for software testers.

Testbytes

5 Broadway, Suite 1101
New York, NY 10006
website: www.testbytes.net

Testbytes is a community of software testers who are passionate about quality and love to test. The site provides articles on various aspects of software testing, including game testing.

Utest

website: www.utest.com

Utest, a community of more than three hundred thousand testers, provides the resources to help testers in their careers. These resources include research on quality assurance tools available, forums to discuss testing, and interviews with those in the quality assurance community.

Writer

What Does a Writer Do?

Video game writers contribute to a video game's design and production. During preproduction (that is, the early portion of a game's development schedule), they help develop the game's plot and characters, flesh out story lines, and create characters' backstories. Game writers closely collaborate with game designers, because every aspect of the video game tells the story, and they need to ensure their writing meets the designer's intent. "Let's say I give a writer the design for a quest," explains David Gaider, designer for games such as *Baldur's Gate 2* and *Knights of the Old Republic*, in a 2016 article on the Polygon website. "I tell them what it's about, what the steps are and who the characters all are, and it's then up to them to flesh it out from that point. They make fewer decisions, but they write everything within the context provided."

In the production phase, writers flesh out the characters, write dialogue, construct details for what occurs within each level, and come up with specific text used in the game for missions, quests, scrolls (game text players read that reveals information about the

At a Glance

Writer

Minimum Educational Requirements
Bachelor's degree preferred

Personal Qualities
Imaginative, detail oriented, organized

Working Conditions
In an office at home or at a gaming studio

Pay
About $36,916 to $72,086

Number of Jobs
About 73,700 for multimedia artists and animators, including game writers, in 2016

Future Job Outlook
Projected 8 percent growth through 2026 for multimedia artists and animators, including writers

level), inventory item descriptions, and cut scenes which are short scenes or movies used to break up the game play. The animators, graphic artists, and programmers use the writing to guide them when creating the characters, items used, and environments within the game. The audio engineers use the dialogue when they record people's voices for the game's characters. Throughout a game's production, writers are expected to edit and revise their work when needed.

George Ziets is the lead area designer for inXile Entertainment's role-playing game *Torment: Tides of Numenera* and has held writing positions on other projects. He believes the key to good writing for a video game is for the writer to have fun when writing and focus on what will engage the player. In an article on the *Forbes* website, Ziets says, "I'm a big believer in the relationship between the writer's fun and the player's entertainment. If the writer is having fun, the player probably will too."

How Do You Become a Writer?

Education
A bachelor's degree or equivalent experience is required to hold a game writer position at a larger and more established game studio. Specifically, creative writing or script writing courses would be helpful for those who aspire to write for video games, as would classes in fiction, storytelling, literature, and narrative voice development. While in high school, students should focus on taking honors or advanced English classes to improve their reading and writing skills.

In addition to obtaining a degree, aspiring game writers should create a portfolio of their writing samples. The portfolio can showcase writing done for a variety of fields—entertainment, newspapers, magazines, and websites. Even with a college degree, most video game writers need to have a portfolio to show to those in the industry. In addition, most game companies require their writers to have at least two years of professional writing experience. Game studios like to see different types of video game writing samples. An example of a sample is writing a quest for a game. Whether the player completes the quest or not results in a different response from the game, and the writer can develop the story as to what will happen and the character's reactions. Game designer and producer David Mullich writes on his personal blog, "The trick to writing a good quest sample is to demonstrate that you can create vivid characters and an engaging plot without writing a lot of backstory or exposition."

Aspiring game writers should also study video game narratives on their own, paying close attention to how the plot unfolds, who the characters are, and what makes the story compelling. "You should eat, breathe and live for video games and love a good story," advises the article "How to Become a Video Game Script Writer," published on the website A Digital Dreamer. "When playing games, pay attention to character development, how a world is presented to the player, and how the dialogue flows. Watch movies, play video games, and read good books."

Volunteer Work and Internships

One way to gain experience and develop a writing portfolio is to volunteer for an independent gaming studio that cannot afford to hire a writer. Search for independent game studios nearby, and volunteer to write for them. Aspiring game writers might also search for unpaid internships on job sites.

To further improve their writing, students can join their school's newspaper or literary clubs, write newsletters, or volunteer to create website content for clubs, churches, and local nonprofit organizations. Additionally, submitting pieces to writing contests of all mediums, such as poetry and fiction, will add to a person's experience and portfolio.

Skills and Personality

A game writer must be flexible, since the requirements for each game and the capabilities of what the game will be able to do are different for every project. For that reason, a game writer has to be able to improvise when needed. Brooke Maggs is a director of

Burning Glass Creative, a company that is contracted to create game design and narrative writing. She says that a writer must understand the time and technical capabilities of the game. "I learnt my lesson early on when I wrote an action packed script for a cutscene, which is a cinematic clip in a game that advances the story," Maggs explains in an article published on the website Aerogramme Writers' Studio. "After presenting it to the team, I was told we only had the time and technical capability to do one simple cutscene. It could involve simple animations like the characters embracing."

Video game writing is by no means a solo endeavor. Game designers are the ones behind the concept for the game, and a writer must always understand the designer's vision and write with it in mind. Writers need to interact with the programmers and animators to clearly implement their story and narrative and then adapt the story based on feedback.

Video games are not like books or short stories, in which the narrative flows from beginning to end. Instead, different choices in a game lead to different results throughout. For example, in the game *80 Days*, a retelling of the novel *Around the World in 80 Days*, players can choose which countries to visit, where to stay while there, and what to do—and these choices impact what will happen next. A video game writer needs to be organized to track all different possible story lines. "The video game player has choices to make, you will need to create flow charts that show the possibilities and variables that the player can face and choose based on their actions," explains the article "How to Become a Video Game Script Writer" on A Digital Dreamer.

On the Job

Employers

For many years, game studios did not hire writers. Instead, game developers and designers wrote their own story lines. But as the game market expanded, developers found they needed higher-quality writing to compete. Today intriguing narratives are considered an essential part of a game, and the larger studios consider writers a necessity. While smaller studios may have to rely on designers to also write the stories, the major game studios can afford to hire whole teams of writers. For example, companies like Impulse Gear and Voltage Entertainment in San Francisco and Warner Brothers in Kirkland, Washington, seek salaried writers and lead writers for their games.

Working Conditions

Smaller studios are more likely to hire just one writer; thus, a game's narrative and character dialogue are likely to be one person's sole responsibility (with input from the designer). In larger studios, a writer is typically assigned a specific area of the game to narrate. "In this case, the work can be more focused," explains video game writer Brian Talbot in the 2016 article "Explainer: The Art of Video Game Writing." He adds, "A writer may write one quest-line (a group of quests or goals that result in a reward and contribute to the story), or the journals of a particular character in the game."

Writers often work on a freelance basis. Therefore, they can set up their office wherever they would like—either at home, in an office space, or in a coworking space. Writers often decorate their work space in ways that inspire them—perhaps by hanging quotes from a favorite book or a game they have worked on. They typically keep their technology simple—game writing only requires a computer or laptop with word processing software.

Earnings

As of September 2018, according to Indeed, the average annual salary for video game writers ranged from $36,916 for a staff writer to $72,086 for a senior writer. This information came from data collected from employees, users, and past and present job advertisements in the thirty-six months prior to that date.

Opportunities for Advancement

A game writer may aspire to become a senior writer at a larger studio. The senior writer is in charge of coordinating all of a game's writing and assigning pieces of script or plot to other writers. He or she then has to ensure that all of the narratives and characters coordinate with each other and that all writers' work is completed on schedule.

Experienced game writers may also aspire to become a game's creative director. The creative director is responsible for the entire vision of the product, including game play, visual style, story, audio assets, cinematics, and marketing materials. To be a successful creative director, one must learn to see the game from the player's perspective. Creative directors must also visualize how the animation, audio, game logic, and story all work together.

What Is the Future Outlook for Writers?

Game writers are included in the category of multimedia specialists and animators by the Bureau of Labor Statistics, which states that in 2016 there were 73,700 of these types of jobs in the United States. From 2016 to 2026 these jobs are expected to show an 8 percent growth due to the increasing popularity of video games in general. Video games are becoming more realistic, with graphics and sound, so developers have found that in-depth stories bring more players to the game. "Video games achieve something that other forms of storytelling just can't," says Dave Gilbert, founder of Wadjet Eye Games, on the website Tech Times. "They put you IN the experience. You are making the events happen, or the events are happening to you. It's not easy to pull off, but when it's done right there is no experience like it." The need for engaging stories adds to the increased need for video game writers. However, it is a competitive field, with many qualified candidates vying for the jobs that are available.

Find Out More

IGDA Game Writing SIG

150 Eglinton Ave. E., Suite 402
Toronto, ON M4P 1E8
website: www.igda.org/group/game-writing

The IGDA Game Writing SIG is made up of game writers, those who hire and work with writers, and those who want to be game writers. Its objective is to build a community of people who write for and about games and to promote the art and craft of writing for the industry.

Richard Dansky

website: www.richarddansky.com

Richard Dansky is a successful fiction and video game writer. His website features a blog about his experiences writing for the video game industry.

Science Fiction and Fantasy Writers of America

PO Box 3238
Enfield, CT 06083
website: www.sfwa.org

The Science Fiction and Fantasy Writers of America promotes, advances, and supports science fiction and fantasy writing by providing resources to aspiring writers. Its website includes information on how to apply for membership and features links to books and articles about writing.

Writers Guild of America West

7000 W. Third St.
Los Angeles, CA 90048
website: www.wga.org

The Writers Guild of America West is a labor union made up of thousands of writers who write all types of media, including video game content. Its website includes articles about the writing craft and features interviews. It also has links to writers' blogs, which provide insight into their projects and processes.

Interview with a Game Producer

Robert Dieterich owns a gaming company, Skyboy Games LLC. He develops and produces independent games and is contracted to port, or adapt, other developers' games from one platform (such as iOS) to another (like Android). Dieterich has over ten years' experience in the video game industry. The author spoke with him via phone about his career.

Q: Why did you become a game producer?
A: Getting the idea to go into game development did not even register as a possibility until in high school when I saw, in a magazine, an article about the game industry. Until then, I did not even know there was a career in games. I saw the article, and knew that was what I would like. After college graduation [with a degree in computer science], I moved to Japan to teach English for a year, and was a freelance programmer. My friend was a games journalist and invited me to a game industry event where I met a person who would eventually become my boss. His company was hiring programmers for games, and I told him I was a programmer.

I spent ten years as a game programmer and as a manager of programmers, working with a variety of platforms, as we went from console to mobile and Android games. Then, I came back to the United States to attend George Mason University for their master of arts game design program. Towards the end of the program, they asked if I'd be interested in teaching, and I became an adjunct professor while still a student, and then an assistant professor after graduation. While doing this, I started developing new games and porting the games of others through my company, Skyboy Games.

Q: Can you describe your typical workday?

A: Right now I am teaching Computer Platform Analysis. The other class I teach is Advance Game Studios. Outside of teaching, I work on my freelance projects. The amount of work I do outside of teaching is determined by time, but I work on them during winter and summer breaks, after hours, and during any free moment. A recent project I worked on is porting a game called *Coup*. People I knew did the iOS version, and asked if I could port it over to Android. This led to other games I also ported to Android. I also have two games on Steam [an online company where games can be bought] that I released through Skyboy Games. One released through SkyBoy is *Ookibloks*, a puzzle game where Ooki the monkey is collecting bananas while avoiding enemies. This was originally an iOS game, which I ported to Mac.

Q: What do you like most about your job?

A: As a professor, I most enjoy working with the students. I like seeing them go at the projects and surprise me with what they develop with the restrictions that I give them. It's satisfying to see them develop and create. As for my own projects, I would go nuts without them and always find time for them. One I enjoyed working on was *Robot Legions Reborn*, a game where the player is fighting against robots. I ported it from Adobe Flash to Xbox Live, and worked to make it feel as though the game was native to the Xbox Live. I also added new bells and whistles, like bigger explosions and the option to control the game using the keyboard or mouse. It was satisfying that the game plays smoothly—as though it was initially made for the new platform.

Q: What do you like least about your job?

A: I do not like the paperwork and documentation, such as contracts and tax forms, required since I own my company. I appreciate the need for it, but I do not like doing it. I do not particularly enjoy anything that involves expense reports. Also, working with a task schedule is not something I hate, but it gives me some dread.

Q: What personal qualities do you find most valuable for this type of work?

A: Creativity, naturally. And, for a lot of games, you need to be able to work with other people. It is not impossible to create games by yourself, but it is limiting. So you need to be able to work effectively, as a part of a team, be open to the ideas of others, and have some humility about your own. Your idea might be solid, but another idea might be just as valid. You also have to have a drive to create. You have to enjoy working out puzzles and finding creative solutions. The people I know who are successful cannot stop themselves from making games—they have a drive to constantly create.

Q: What is the best way to prepare for this type of job?

A: You do not necessarily need a game design degree, but it can help. While you do learn software, like Unity and 3ds Max, for game design at school, I specifically work on teaching students how to learn. You have to be able to learn on your own in the industry because new technology is constantly emerging, and chances are companies in the industry will be using different software than you were taught in school.

Q: What other advice do you have for students who might be interested in this career?

A: You have to be a self-learner. Get out there and download the free tools that are available, like Unreal Engine or Unity. Install them, look at their websites, and do the tutorials. Then start creating. The big mistake is to think, "I shouldn't learn these tools until I'm in a game design program." It's a race from day one, so start learning now. Build something!

Other Jobs in Online Gaming

Assistant producer

Associate creative director

Broadcast engineer

Chief executive officer
   of a game studio

Contest designer

Creative director

Customer support agent

DevOps engineer

Digital media correspondent

Engine programmer

External producer

Game recruiter

Lead programmer

Level editor

Lighting artist

Marketing manager

Multimedia artist

Musician

Narrative copywriter

Project manager

Server engineer

Software developer

Sound designer

System designer

Technical artist

3-D modeler

Translator

User interface artist

Video editor

Voice actor

Editor's note: The US Department of Labor's Bureau of Labor Statistic provides information about hundreds of occupations. The agency's *Occupational Outlook Handbook* describes what these jobs entail, the work environment, education and skill requirements, pay, future outlook, and more. The *Occupational Outlook Handbook* may be accessed online at www.bls.gov/ooh.

Index

Picture Credits

About the Author

Leanne K. Currie-McGhee has been an educational writer for nearly fifteen years. She lives with her husband, Keith, her daughters Grace and Hope, and her fur baby, Delilah.